The National Poetry Series was established in 1978 to ensure the publication of five collections of poetry annually through five participating publishers. The series is funded annually by Amazon Literary Partnership, the Gettinger Family Foundation, Bruce Gibney, HarperCollins Publishers, Tabitha and Stephen King Foundation, Lannan Foundation, Newman's Own Foundation, Anna and Olafur Olafsson, Penguin Random House, the Poetry Foundation, Elise and Steven Trulaske, and the National Poetry Series Board of Directors.

2022 Competition Winners

Organs of Little Importance
by Adrienne Chung
Chosen by Solmaz Sharif for Penguin Books

Tender Headed
by Olatunde Osinaike
Chosen by Camille Rankine for Akashic Books

Survival Strategies
by Tennison S. Black
Chosen by Adrienne Su for University of Georgia Press

I Love Information
by Courtney Bush
Chosen by Brian Teare for Milkweed Editions

Sweet Movie
by Alisha Dietzman
Chosen by Victoria Chang for Beacon Press

I LOVE

INFORMATION

I LOVE INFORMATION

poems

COURTNEY BUSH

MILKWEED EDITIONS

Published 2023 by Milkweed Editions
Printed in Canada
Cover design by Mary Austin Speaker
Cover artwork: "Mocking of Christ," by Fra Angelico, 1441. Pictures Now / Alamy Stock Photo.
Author photo by Jake Goicoechea
23 24 25 26 27 5 4 3 2 1
First Edition

Library of Congress Cataloging-in-Publication Data

Names: Bush, Courtney, author.
Title: I love information : poems / Courtney Bush.
Other titles: I love information (Compilation)
Description: First edition. | Minneapolis, Minnesota : Milkweed Editions,
   2023. | Summary: "I Love Information is a vigorous examination of
   knowledge, belief, and which begets which"-- Provided by publisher.
Identifiers: LCCN 2023001102 (print) | LCCN 2023001103 (ebook) | ISBN
   9781639550036 (trade paperback) | ISBN 9781639550029 (ebook)
Subjects: LCGFT: Poetry.
Classification: LCC PS3602.U8357 I2 2023 (print) | LCC PS3602.U8357
   (ebook) | DDC 811/.6--dc23/eng/20230414
LC record available at https://lccn.loc.gov/2023001102
LC ebook record available at https://lccn.loc.gov/2023001103

Milkweed Editions is committed to ecological stewardship. We strive to align our book production practices with this principle, and to reduce the impact of our operations in the environment. We are a member of the Green Press Initiative, a nonprofit coalition of publishers, manufacturers, and authors working to protect the world's endangered forests and conserve natural resources. *I Love Information* was printed on acid-free 100% postconsumer-waste paper by Friesens Corporation.

this book is for my friends

Contents

I LOVE

INFORMATION

WHEN YOU GET TO SPARTA VOICE

I do not want to be crazy
about the circle whose center is everywhere.
The metallic parts of mind drawn to an image of the spill,
one that goes wine and wine and more wine. A friend is gone
and I wanted to be all blade, too scary to use.

Where the intuitive paths people took before us
rubbed the grass away from the dirt at the top corner of the park,
what's wrong with you?
You seemed combinedly possessed by every robin that fell.

I am expected to write about the art I've been looking at.
Well the story in Wagner was only the summary of a story.

In summer I arrived at the idea of entering sacred time recklessly
as it regarded the way men interpreted the behaviors of my friend Jessa and me.
We walked home from Del Taco saying you snap, then I'll snap.
She pulled her tampon out behind the dumpster while the Scientology cross burned.
The strongest member of our party had gone overboard.
Of course not everything is about that.

To yellow-haired Helen, I really liked you, I thought you were amazing.
The way you threw away the pretty napkin we got with the takeout.
The little cockroach on the lip of the stove then the lip of the sink
going around the whole room with complete freedom.

I wanted you to be happy like that, where I could see you
and my sight at times had no limit. As a visionary I was a loser.
My spinal cord always filled up with whatever chemicals felt like
the other world had already rejected me.

If you give me the chance, I'll hold the handful of egret feathers by the gate,
wave long goodbye, smile with teeth like lemon seeds, I don't care, at this point,
I understand exactly half of everything.

In Los Angeles there was fake blood ponding in the ring. There was someone cool
to drink the blood. A dove drunk on mulberries. There was the underworld
of learning which is not beautiful, not the ugly beauty of a model even.
There was instead a path of decimation upon which all you could do was submit.

LATE PREAMBLE

My thing that year
was believing in things

There would be a lost pilot
An internal logic in each event

It was easy with the children. We found money for Elsa from *Frozen*. Plastic chess pieces gathered in arrangements on the floor. Ten of the kids piled scarves over the bodies of the two smallest as they lay on the floor playing dead. A pink then a red scarf fell. They told me as I approached, before I even asked

These are our bodies and we said it was okay.

When the adults showed me in word and action what they cared about, it was harder to imagine there was some internal logic strong enough to believe in, but I did it.

I was the dad who can sing
Pain is the lost pilot
and I was the lost pilot
and I was the person
who had come a long way
with arms outstretched
from the famous poem
and I was the cowboy

and that year turned into many years

KATELYN

1

Fucked-up Greek movie on Easter Sunday

Mulberries made the doves drunk

Kite's foot was a reedlike grass

How are you supposed to be survived

Grief does not make us weaker

But it might not make us strong like they said

I love when celebrities cry on Instagram

Like I love my first love

And life in my eyes then outside them

My house dying for the Lord to come

In the form of a nonlinear accumulation

In the synopsis you are described as a vulnerable screenwriter

But you tried to strangle the fiancé you proposed to yesterday

When I couldn't hear the sink running

Singing so loud in the shower I'll fly away in the morning

If I die Hallelujah by and by

Starting from the top until my house had flooded

2

Concerning the bartender Jef with one *f*

It was like the Middle Ages and I was like the angel

Talking to Molly who was trying to work

I'm back I said

Maybe it was only my kink radar speaking

A kink angel with a recitation just the same as the other kind

Looking like a Mylar balloon in the yard

I would calm down if it weren't for the risk of dislocating my personality

You've written beautifully about your manic episode

What wonderful things to believe

There is always reason to stop a sentence

But no structural obligation

I want to smell like Rachael Leigh Cook smelled

In the scene where they go to prom

I want to smell like a Roman centurion

I had this lazy baseless idea I would go back to writing regular poetry

3

My boyfriend's brother does the voice-over

On a half-hour television show about animal rehabilitators

Called *Hope in the Wild*

Brittany watched it while she ate tomato pie

I put bronzer on my face saying

Bronzer is the velvet of the face

The disgusting seal who keeps trying to escape

In the third episode quickly became my North Star

The cycles of love and torment coming faster

Small and in my heart

Last night propped up on one arm to delete larger files

To free memory in my phone and saw the cat

A month before the divorce

Follow me along the counter

The thin strip of fake granite by the sink

I sat up crying afraid of the bad dreams that would come

But from the dream that came I woke up laughing

About the way my student wrote his last name on a star

A red paper star like in a car lot

And everyone in your dreams is you

So you never know the you you are

And you're the only one who does

4

I began to see all art is about organization

Yes, all of it

And the portrait show seems to have no faces

Only the deeply ingrained human need

To make useless things

Everybody makes mistakes

That's what this shirt is about

I called Anne-Louise, my anxious student

The loudest opera recording played in her house

Her mom said Anne-Louise can't talk right now

She's giving birth to animals

There she was in the background on the floor

Her mom in dangling elaborate earrings said

Anne-Louise made me wear these

We are making soup out of Play-Doh

Anne-Louise drank the purple water we rinsed the cabbage with

I play along but know that of all the children

This lifestyle could break Anne-Louise

Who wants to count the circle crackers on each child's napkin

Who needs to help me pass out the snack

Who can't sleep at rest time because she is so excited to have a job

But I'm not lucky

My fear is that I will forget to do everything my fear

Is that my love is weak

What will I do when my little students start organizing the world this way

Anne-Louise did once write a poem, though not an alarming one

Only mimicking the organization that will ruin your life

It was about eating a rainbow

Then Mikey lying on the floor said I'm writing a poem about circles

And we saw

a circle has 0 sides

but I can't

have 0 things

5

I had my second revelation

The thought planted in my head in usable language when I woke from sleep

Was not a novel idea

We are supposed to recreate our lives the way a little child would

Inside the realm of your imagination

And the small realm of your control

Pronoun incongruity is retained because it was a revelation

I do not love the revelation

Which pretends to know the way a child's mind works

So many adults do that

Even I talk to the children this way sometimes I say

We aren't yelling today, my love

When that's clearly what we are doing

The people who made up that revelation

Are the same people who think every kid likes the Beatles

We make our own music here

Oh my word / I love that bird

All the same it was my revelation

If someone else has a revelation I get to keep mine

I have had a revelation

And I will have no other worry

Well I have one

My love being weak

KATELYN

These aren't blueberries

and teeth have their own minds

A fragment of truth hasn't been put in the lie

Do you feel the centipede I feel in me

Is the Emerson in your mirror young as the one in mine

The first buildings were trees

The percent of you that wants to die fluctuates

when something good happens

The best buildings were bodies

You solved a small mystery at your high school

You committed four crimes in the West

Someone you know has been reading Machiavelli all summer

Noticing TV's disquieting remove

You could no longer imagine a future

I could've sat down and cried with you

That could've been my clearest memory

JUBILATE AGNO

I feel like all I have is a brain

You keep making mistakes over and over, Lauren

Shirts that changed colors

Garbage bags that sat in burning fires without melting

You don't even support the town

A music teacher shops late at Walmart

In a sweatshirt covered in little fish

In the middle of an incurable nervous breakdown

I took my mother to the play and in the play

I killed Greg's girlfriend without consulting a script

For the first five hours I was a vehicle of pure consciousness

Trucks were seen in garages and then not seen in garages

Metal handcuffs left no marks on the bedposts

The fire in the gorge began and ended at different times

I found mysticism in a ranch-style house

Countlessly wished at the top of the stairs

Crossed the yard walked through the gate

Walked through the brown grass up to my knees

Past the Planned Parenthood through the Planned Parenthood parking lot

Cried into the eastbound traffic and then

Chased Peter right into it raging bright red

Chased Josh into the headlit traffic too

Then all my friends came running

I had said come back and they came back

Even from the dead, rising from the knee-length lawn

Where I had tried to pick out all the glass

Their bodies in the weak green light

I asked Greg's girlfriend to come back and she came back

And onto the highway light, streams of it

Meeting and dispersing

The one that hit me with his truck came back

The one who called me bitch came back

The one who broke into my house

Who took our cat and renamed her and lied

The one I loved while fire melted my boot soles

Who impaled his hands on a barbed-wire fence

Ending up with stigmata at Kelli's farm

He's back waving white arms on the esplanade

Do you think you're better than me

Do you live in New York City

One punch to the face on the front lawn

One body through a barbecue grill on the back porch

One frozen burrito in the microwave

One drunk and naked girl screaming

One drunk in fetal position in the soccer goal

One fallen mailbox, one pile of bricks, one scratch filled in with nail polish

As everything with angels is nine

Down the stairs in a pillowcase

Bloody legs in the woods

Somebody looking in the window

Somebody else lighting napkins

My mother's friend Michael came back

Instead of a name an epiphany

The weed came back when the money came back

When we lost it, it was found

Tess came back saying the whole sky is cold

Your arms full of books came back

Jameson crept back to my room to read one more poem

We opened a window and the crow came back

Into the apartment where we had to kill it

And its body drained into the highway behind the house

Brown leaves drain backward, aluminum cans thrown in the woods

Drawn back a yard at a time

The creek itself moving back and back

The crack of a twig in the middle of the night

Zach came back believing in UFOs

Eating french fries

Blake came back vomiting on a puddle of ice

You came back making mistakes over and over, Lauren

You came with your phone lit up in the hand behind your back

Lighting one line of you

Lighting a few bleached hairs whipping in the noise

Gabriel came back with a nose full of poison berries

Lucas came back with a peach

Before the baby was born, she kept coming back

Draining herself into the lonely yellow highway strip

Treating it like a bowl

And how many times I've said I'll never dance again

How many times I've become a trout in a fish stream

The magic drained from me

The animals with no magic

The conversation I repeated this time lacked all magic

The water drained from the man-made lake

The sand dredged up from the middle of the sea to build a beach

In the middle of the impossibly loud highway

Loud every hour of every life

Television created the illusion of you coming back

When it was also real

And real my mother coming back on the illusion of a forked poem

One fork in my bedroom, the last poem Jameson read saying

The lyric itself is too much

One fork a path into a world of sin

I was told we'd be taken somewhere placid

I was told the highway ended north

And south you could drive straight into the Gulf

Dovetailing, you came back

Dovetail, into the highway under the big lights

For you, they change them out for stadium lights

Hunting lights, police spotlights, a light you could mount on a submarine

A car with high beams, honking as it flew

KATELYN

The wind pattern they call snake came back
The football player they call snake came back
Rozz orders fennel with a champagne vinaigrette

The memoir the Valentine's Day in the empty
Apartment dancing to harvest
Moon and I was crying in a world of ultraviolet light

Is this the rapture or is it not
The good fire eating the bad fire
This far in the woods not only
Is there a house, there's a person coming out of it

An empty soda bottle at the edge of a creek
At the edge of a public park with the used broken condoms
Has two faces better than the moon's and more distinct
Sun-bleached and perfect orange, perfect purple

You are the leech angel

Remembering with perfect clarity a Chinese restaurant in Yonkers

On your deathbed, recalling slumlord oak-colored

Fake wood cabinets going all the way around the room

Like a leech angel

KATELYN

Three angel Windsor

Triple angel Lutz

She found out there are only three kinds of ovens

Sweaters finish drying on chairs

What is there left to care about

My boss says my ex's ex looks like a mushroom

The new one like an Olsen twin with wet tangled hair

The sky is annoying

You couldn't call this snowfall

Desire is good for songs movies and poetry

Swann wasn't able to strategically harness it

These are not the blueberries

You pretend I am

I am a door-to-door maniac

And certainly not to love you now

Or more

Or creatively

KATELYN

When I passed the church it was the Middle Ages

When they said hello it was the Middle Ages even more

I girded my face with the wool of my coat's sleeve

I made it steellike and wandered down into a cave

Customers who come in contact with trains enter saint mode

They practice flapping

The spoiled quest of making noise

I ignored the angels

So my children took their paths into a world of eternal punishment

And my husband does not believe in true love

And the child I mention is so kind it makes me angry

One poet said we write this way to forget

All contradiction made for forgetting

All grass the condition of flesh

But to forget is an abstract concept

Nobody owns the meaning of these things

People do not speak in sentences

We are not made alive to sentences alone

DIED SINGING

At 9 a.m. holding a sponge bloated with soap and water
I burst into tears imagining my life without the constant torment
Of my relationship with alcohol
My arms became weak and more realizations entered
About what I was afraid of
What was beautiful in my village
What gave stories necessity
It was the personality I have
Oh it was myself
John Cassavetes knew something about me
In all those scenes when someone forces someone else to sing
There is a dark interpretation to the sweetest song
The children gathering seaweed
The unreliable narrator you follow to the riverbed
Reading meaning in the garbage
Flowers growing in the garbage
My heart has been totally eclipsed with an unhealthy need

Through the countryside I've been dragging this shovel
I will drag until I find the right clay for building a bell

My hero designed the ugliest restaurant I've ever laid eyes on
My captain told me I'm only a transmitter for other things
Feed the dogs
Give the demons to the pigs
Wear a simple garment
God will forgive you
That's not your job

I love these drums
I am so pure of heart I didn't believe in evil until it befell me
Women gather at the fountain
Small radios hung from their necks
Men laid down to rest on rugs with intricate patterns
Kim said she has learned remarkable things by living
Receiving hostility with no motivation
Transmitting
Withstanding forces of love
The clay became pliable as my hands warmed it
More red than brown
Many hands dedicated their heat to the red bell
In dreams I pursued the bell until my waking life took on the quality of a ringing
The contour of all sounds added pressure
Under which I was compelled to submit
To the sharp rim of the bell
The tongue inside it being swung by a strong angry man
With ginger on his breath

It comes down to a few things
Vessels and bags
Every crude tool
Every day a friend to tell
Raphael's fresco
The two angels flanking
And his manic episode a few years ago
And you're told they have the knowledge of the causes of things
And they tell you where to look
And you're told to have fun with it
You there at the limits
Having your breakdown in the kitchen with the whole day ahead

KATELYN

For money
I illustrated a book on horse surgery with my closest friend
buttered bread and put it on a hot slab of iron
I wiped vomit from Coco's chest
I watched the blood gathering there
I was so sentimental I had to believe he was alive
I wrote one hundred knock-knock jokes about Easter
made cheese out of nuts
washed reusable paper towels in the sink of a rich woman
wrote lines that did not orbit pool or curve
I folded onesies into diamond shapes
I agreed to call the department when I saw bruises
and came so far from what I actually felt
I lied about where the soup came from
I crushed chickpeas to a fine mist
I dyed tap water with natural food color
and helped a child touch the water
I let a sinister guinea pig's teeth penetrate my fingertip

To establish dominance
I read six books at once
I admitted my obsession to my obsession
walked fearlessly into the wild sweep of corn
I screamed louder and stood when I wanted to sit

I made cookies from a tube

I restricted calories, I ran and ran and squatted and planked

I understood everything

I remembered the shape of every vestibule

I listened for the crack of a twig

I practiced archery at a sordid camp in Alabama

told the teacher opossum starts with an O

I got in trouble

I doodled on the script

I held the knives

I dug deep grooves into what I had done

I dissolved the inferior materials and left the gold

I engineered a virus spread by insect

I read Machiavelli all summer to get back at the one who read Machiavelli all summer

I painted Merritt Parkway

Before that I invented permanent green

Between the invention and the painting I popularized the color

I redirected traffic and fixed everything

I trained my dog to kill the police

to kill the president

I told Tom not to follow his heart because his heart is a piece of shit

RILKE VOICE

I remember having no control
More difficult than any angel wherever she may be caught
In whatever breast in whatever
Blue pink yellow light
In gladiator light

*

The prodigy I held so close
I said close to her heart her country reminds me of Y2K
Even then it shouldn't be Glenn Gould all the time
Mary Robison, the second elegy at Duino or the computer
Plus whatever I had to say to you a year ago

*

Singing *Turandot* at night in the snow
Singing *Turandot* outside like a bot
To all the rich people dressed as punks on the train at rush hour
The angel's stuck in a hole in a leaf

Snagged on some edge
Like when I try to remember everything I love
And love is back

*

That Connecticut lady won't shut up
Less than a year has passed
And it will happen again

I would tell you about it
Pushing you to Antarctica
In the free museum wheelchair
Being so mean to you

*

We can't deny back there we felt closer
To where we are going than now
When we saw the painting with the angels in the rafters
You said that one is just a spear of light
The others were babies
Parts of babies with wings
A head
And you said we are happier than they are
Than everyone
And it felt like standing on a cliff

*

Half the time Coco doesn't understand the words themselves
Half the time only meaning eludes her
I feel inside I will transform
And you can justify anything by connecting it to Ashbery
There is no one to talk me out of it
As one of us has to eat, clean, receive and give away money

*

If a photograph exists
It can't really be rare
At Duino I could call on something Italian too
My mom's friend Carmine

From the middle of the Earth
The sin-cake eater
I'm fighting over who should buy the cigarettes

*

What's the youngest you've ever been
And the youngest you could bear being again

At Duino I could isolate looking for you from abstract looking
And on top of the hand is the underhand

*

I miss other people more
They are hosing things down
So smart
So today when they hose down the chicken warehouses
I'd like to be a complete idiot or a complete anything
In the first clips of sunlight

*

In the sun is a metal circle
Turning into a dance that goes around
There is a premonition in language of the never-ending pain
Eclipsing itself
Out on the moors
It fractures and that is totally fine
On the moors
The female schooner captain died today
The gay cool female schooner captain

*

Katelyn said not that road
There will be a morning
And a road that makes you feel better about yourself

*

Dancing with the romaine lettuce devil
Sitting on the seawall with the man who killed the mayor
Emily Dickinson's Poems: As She Preserved Them
I told Andy he had these and other unspeakably dark forces to thank
For all the LA modern architecture he's obsessed with
That's how drunk I was
Mitya Pyotr 1 Pyotr 2 Dmitri Petroshka Your Name
I do this to myself

*

Listening to music and watching TV at the same time is impossible
A teenager told his girlfriend on the train this morning
Trying to fill holes
Frantic and ecstatic must come from the same place
When you take out the Christian myths
The angels are still in the rafters
Hanging over the empty barn
Stray clumps of hay
Dust
A dog

*

If one person can sing three songs at once
There could be more songs than ears

If you want to be hysterically funny
Write out the logic of anything

*

When I sing I'm just saying
The question does the begging
People are not special
Being alive is special

Leonard Cohen yelling
In the end we give up customs we barely had time to learn
That is what hysterical light made me think

*

Goodnight my love
I am trying to read six books at once
Some people change and some don't
That is not a literary device
Some people learn something
1-800-HURT
In this way it is like a garden
Or an aquarium where some flowers live by accident
There is nothing spectacular about a show of hands
Fuck a Whitmanic list
I always say
We are supposed to somehow give things to each other
Without taking anything away

*

I saw a kid dabbing and flossing
At the Hilma af Klint show
I told my preverbal children how nighttime is pointless
I read the *Elegies* at the top of my lungs
And yes they cried out for someone else

*

Lost beyond the resources of talk
I took the path of things so mysterious we shouldn't bother with explaining
To play a heavy metal song of love
Fires
When I asked is there not something like Greek tragedy
But now

*

I pursued my obsession with shame and confusion
He is a nice person and he's not using drugs anymore
So that's even better
So you feel what I want maybe it could be transitive
Oh no
This is what I meant about not taking anything away
Silver at the gills with facts about the Cold War
Silver in the bouncy balls at Walmart

*

To the bridge that fell
You were the worst bridge

*

Something to suck water out of the ground
Intimate like the only self
They are out there, along the highway
In summer
My mom called me an evil weed-smoking thug
And you're distracted talking to a friend in the backseat
About nothing in particular
A child who knows poems is just a child who knows poems
Already too many of those

Something was lying to you

*

The youngest thing you could imagine
Give me a gold coin

When I sing I'm just trying to make a dog cry

POEM AFTER MY FIRST REVELATION

I'm it   I'm not a part of it
It is a narrative of immaculate control. Marjorie,
by meeting me in my experience of reality imprints
what she could've only said in person: Everything is a choice.

She would've decided this to be the most predictable moment
for the rest of my life, here at Andrew's house, choosing
not to wear shoes outside to sit on the bench. I heard, Looks like
somebody doesn't have shoes on. It was a choice.

Andrew operates as light from a dead star

says if I learned anything from Marjorie Welish it's everything is a choice

and the work is done in a mechanism we are fools in believing
taught by nature's incoherence, the disorder of how leaves fall how
sometimes the bank is just closed and same, each other. In ways
the outside might know down into each self, and dimly
inharmonious with not.

I received a revelation, I will have no other worry

I don't think about it

Sitting in Delaware beyond the revelation, I will have no other worry

I don't think it

The revelation is that this narratological
structure is included in the perfect disorder.

The point of this narrative, as particular fatal intervention
arches back over the looseness of a friendship, a time spent
in schools, and swallows, joins the river returning to bare feet
the song of Marjorie's maxim, it is not the narrative, but that
the structure exists, that it is possible

It is not thinking it which I do

That these should not be tercets, but they would not be tercets,
and it never goes back to the way it was, if someone else gets
a revelation I keep mine.

Across the marble countertop someone says he is just getting started.
To say started on the comparative outskirt of life's first moment
after revelation, nothing could start. In bed I can't explain this,
I feel like the revelation is going to text me, it feels different.
Life after having the revelation is not receiving
the revelation. How is life after. Slow, the holy
emerging fit for use. Not because of the revelation and not despite it,
it's not that good. It is just between, it is alongside.
I give a value judgment to prepositions
because they have them.

CASSANDRA FROM *AGAMEMNON* VOICE

Do you think the angel of death looks like Beetlejuice
One child asked another in the bent part of the bus
In a heaven of facts without context, clean sources of light
When there's nothing more complex to worry about
If you've seen these lines before, it was a different day
They discontinued Doodleheads
They brought them back
Joy was not less pathetic than the worst grief
This is how I communicate now
In relationships romantic in the art historical sense
This moment I am less the wife and more the man
Telling my wife not to touch me
Blue light changed to red on a timer
The fight sounded like *Jesus was a man but not really...*
I think music is always proof
The end of summer the erratic bees
Know they're about to die
I looked sideways at a friend's notes from his ego death
Who stopped speaking to me when I said I didn't need one
I told my boyfriend sobriety doesn't rupture so he would not be afraid
When someone says poetry is silence I will lose
Because it's not true but makes everyone's life easier
I will lose to other women
I will lose even harder to freedom
I don't want to be better than I am
Chocolate cake ground into the floor of the bus
Sprinkles like it was a birthday at my feet
I left all my friends at Tatiana Grill
Two were so in love I couldn't look them in the eyes
If what made sense was to focus, I would have no problem doing that

Having come from so far away to end up somewhere even further
The right to fragment
The worst every year is when a poet dies
To have the idea of the secret chord is to have the secret chord
And we have it

MY SON IS HOME

Possessing only a brain does not serve you well

It does not serve you well in love

There's a catfight in the rain

Because people love an underworld story

In Australia Tinder's name is Gumtree Classifieds

So I put my brain there

The two options for leaving me

And water covers the slabs in sheets

And the sheets are dirty

My divorce like all events

Did not happen in one tense or another

I miss wanting to be touched

I miss not hating voices

I actually don't miss my husband

Payton was drunk, I was drunk

We watched the blood girl collect her billions

In my apartment so shitty except for the skylight

Picking up everything

In the living room the light finding you for once

So you can think with your higher mind

I don't want to know the names for anything

Not one bird, tree, plant

I've already said how much I don't like mountains

Once I learned plums and peaches are drupes

Knowing a bird's name I would overflow with rage

That and the plums, it's happening now

Is it clear I want to know people's names only

Phil, Margaret, Nehemiah, Clare

I love when someone says my name

And know it doesn't make the world any better

At least I know love is the point of everything

So love is why stingrays kill people

For a while I pretended to believe in a female god figure

Due to the zeitgeist

But I believe women are all the same

And men too

At this time I can only handle being almost stupid

And my glassy underfed eyes make me look closer to death

On the good side which is to say young

Remember when he was just so funny

His blond curls and thinking how did I get here

The same way old movies begin

The way new movies end

So love is why you aren't supposed to lean on the doors

Of my desire I've been keeping this short list

Realism in film so pure it causes mass insanity

And deep psychological punishment

PENELOPE VOICE

Completely obsessed with flowers. I made all these
ovals and lines about my house filling up
with flowers.

Things you say are falling robins from the song.
Heavy, not dispersing like the light on half a stadium of heads.

None of this was the surprise.
Not parts going out of control.
Not the parts that needed my care.
Those turning out to be the same parts,
finding out they didn't want to be touched
was the surprise.

Alone I picked the glass out of the lawn,
the sharp edges digging for the substratum,
so friends could lie down on the wet grass
tilting beer cans to their lips. Still they never catch up.

My student writes her name on the back of her paper
though she can't make any letters.
Her faint but constant series of ovals and lines
says Penelope and I can read it. She can read it
though she can't read.
I will recognize that set of lines and ovals,
the same one she makes every day once she's gone home
and I'm going through the stacks of watercolors.
This one says Penelope.
If I saw it in a thousand years.

I hate when singers can really sing like I hated
when you took my hand in your hand,
took me out in the rain
to tell me what you don't really think.
By that time I had had enough of the half-oracular.
When the third thing in the prophecy doesn't come true
but you're still on the cursed boat
wondering what to do with the fourth thing.
Its mutated fate-body thrown on the deck
more realistic than you expected.

There was a creek behind my sister's house I loved
for how stupid it made me feel
not because I believe nature is omniscient,
I don't, and I don't go there anymore.
My friends drunk riding 4-wheelers
into power lines don't really go away.
I rejoiced in the lamb. I was asked
was I real or fake,
did I prefer Ashley or Mary-Kate?
Men said I love you but meant
they had done something wrong which I would find out about later,
broke into my house, cracked the Italian figurines
when they swung their long legs over the back of the couch.
I waited on the curb for someone named Brock to pick me up.
I wondered if a sword could blaze.

With the TV on like my mother before me I descend to dreams.
One poem says TV is what the night eats.
Writing is what the dreams eat.
My growing concern was that the instant
was not the unit of experience that interested me.
The woman made of static said I'm scared of everyone.

The woman gathering asters in the ravine
stays there unwilling to go either up the mountain home
or down to face the animals she knows wait for her
the night we had the pink moon to distract us,
no docents orbiting the central fountain.

I want to tell you what a sword is.
To want to tell you has been my entire life.
And writing is the same thing as waiting.
And talking is as useful as it sounds.

KATELYN

Don't remove me from your favors

Black couch and heavy grain of the footage

This can't happen to somebody else

For the first five hours I was glued to the screen

I told myself I didn't like exploitation

Tempted to give the plants coffee

She is stuck in me

If you like parking lots you will love a junkyard

She is stuck in me (the angel in the breast light)

You would be sad, stuck, nature took back the car yard

Deep stream, brain fingerprinting

I thought that future was going to go to the end

Narrative can be provided by anyone

But I want yours, it's yours I want

You are a formless water dying easily

And something has been troubling my husband in his sleep

I will become a trout in a fish stream

Hit the wall, track it into the house

So if dying is easy I will probably never die

SERAPHIM OR NOTHING

In a dream the man I'm more or less in love with for a year
sent me a photo of an action painting behind glass in the reflection of which
I can see a woman in his bed I recognize from the internet
though we have no reason to talk in my waking life
he sends me stills from a Kathryn Bigelow movie
I can't imagine being about anything other than
being beautiful and silent for a long time
The lights on the 18-wheeler mean it's coming toward me
Love is how I always wanted it
The children trust me and say take us out of this mess
Sonnet it's time for you to do what you said you would
I'm talking to you now
You will do this for me
You will think

To be here with so much flesh
Elvira was saying
and violence in one place
is just great
I used to believe everything
was either all real or all fake
That was being younger
so the things my boyfriend did confused me
and much greater and more important things
happening around me passed without my grasping
Alright well thank you and welcome
to WrestleMania 2 love from Los Angeles
love from the Tower of Song

Megan and I walked around the block
Sam's dad died
I told her my thoughts felt so balanced
they could do some kind of physical work
as strong as a crane or a thousand teenagers
Could level a field
She thought I meant witchcraft
She wanted me to talk to Sam
like I could help him do some
I remember when he wanted to start a militia
Men can't do witchcraft I told her
It's why all old songs are about
pretty women drowning
You can't have everything

Friend is the name I use in the preschool
when I want the children to know
what I am telling them
is only based on our context
not on who we are
so not based on the way
whenever I speak one on one
to a certain friend
she tucks my hair behind my ear
in a gesture of the love
that is coming back to me
a gesture of the complete circle of it
I have to believe it's possible to set this up
to listen and to talk at the same time

Two Easters ago I looked down
at a bunny my mother made on the stone countertop
from a round loaf of Hawaiian bread
by carving the middle out
and using that part to form ears
then filling the hole with some kind of dip
then pressing m&m's into the bread for eyes
After she made the bunny she told me
she had invited her newly dead boyfriend's sons
who none of us had ever met
to come that night to read the will
in the same room as that bunny
I remember thinking these are the kinds of memories I'll have
and the two m&m's weren't even the same color

I told Megan it didn't matter
how obsessed Sam was with witchcraft
because even his most true obsession
would not compare to the least of mine
which are still built on the kind of attention
passed down from the beginning of time
having to do with the connection
between survival and focus
unlike his obsession
which would center
on survival and I don't know what
There is only one shoulder
I ever needed to memorize
Nothing happened but I memorized it

I was drunk drinking thin blue
calorie-less Powerade with Aristocrat vodka
in the soccer goal in the yard
with Sarah and Justin
This is the story of my first kiss
I didn't believe in an interventionist god
The plants inside the house were dead
though my mom fed them
the Tab she swore by
and inside mine are dying
though I feed them coffee
the closest thing I have
She said it will be pretty funny
when we are both 33 in heaven

I know when one friend says
I'm not tired she should get a book
but when another friend says I'm not tired
he needs me to come over
with the weighted blanket
to pat his chest and talk in a low voice about what he loves
I know the pattern:
be afraid to be left alone only to be left alone
the audiobook in the stereo
Frog and Toad eating all cookies
The children scared of sharks ask what I'm scared of
I am scared I won't find the lost pilot
I am scared I'll forget to do everything
and what that friend loves is drums

I broke a friend's name
or the spell my voice had cast when I said his name
up to that point when I screamed it (Noah)
when I saw him jabbing his little index finger
at the reset button on the electrical outlet
I knew I could
by screaming his name scare him
in a way it was important I had never before
You know this in an emergency
You access strategies
and I wished I hadn't had to do that
and told him how I wished I hadn't had to do that
and remembered once he had misunderstood some logistical aspect of the day
and asked then who is going to take care of us

A really seductive commercial
selling refrigerators on Brittany's TV
has anchored its mission in how precious figs are
so the woman slowly cuts the figs in half
before placing them on the glass platform
inside the fridge's main chamber and hopes
they will remain safe but become colder
I have to buy celery and food coloring for an experiment
Someone on Twitter has been talking to the dead
Every three or four days
Reality is obsessive
The number of days since you smoked your last cigarette is intimate
I read in a children's book
that fairies have no pity

The Egyptian *Book of the Dead* is called
the book of coming into the day
In it I read one morning
we are living in the filth of Osiris
Felt I had read some eternal truth
as life might as well be and have been and continue to be
the filth of Osiris and found it a little funny
like what death is like for the dead is funny
because we have absolutely no perspective
I always loved how you learn
the rhythm of jokes
but never what they are
It's slow and has no end like waking
phasers set to the impersonal world

When I was drunk in high school
I would peel the shrink-wrap
from a frozen salmon fillet
from a Sam's Club bulk bag in the kitchen
lit only by the freezer light
put it unseasoned in a teal frosted plastic bowl
directly into the microwave which
when I opened it
created a second light
a light from above
and heat the fish on high
for as long as it took
to make it hot and I liked the way it tasted
I thought it was good

I listen to everything Jeesoo says
and she said from the end of the coffee table
she thought everything in my poem was true
Only then did it occur to me
while I used my hand to move pistachio shells around a plate
that it might not be
that to write about things I had experienced was not the only option
and I do remember many things
and I want to give my brain something it wants
but it would be interesting
and make a kind of sense
if what I wanted to give my brain didn't exist
I understand the structure of the world
as a person being interrupted but not in a bad way

I tried making an expansive neurological tissue
with sonnets that overlapped
in which any 3 consecutive stanzas
each having 4 or 5 lines would touch each other
in ways that added up to 12–15 lines
The idea was based on the sonnet's reputation
for solving and my serious intention
to make a poem that can think
It was less a formal exercise than a spell
I was counting on to work or else why live
That's what I was always saying to Brittany before the children got to school
and that poem was long and bad
because that idea was no good
That poem wouldn't think but it was almost thinking

In a Quaker meeting in Pasadena
a man told an old story
about a friend in the Quaker sense of the word
called to sail from America to England
to attend a meeting at his old meetinghouse
who on arrival was so filthy
no one recognized him as a friend
how that was the worst thing he ever felt
I told Paul in the cemetery the story of the story
when I was feeling very emotional
and about how if I asked someone to draw the scene
so much would be left out
the blue tarp the pile of cans the car on cinder blocks the garbage and shit
the story of the story of the worst feeling

Writing is so often treated like some ravenous villain
of the actual world
but I don't believe it makes anything worse
I don't like the way songs define god
by saying all the things god is not
because what they actually identify
is some baseline fear
that there just isn't anything
I don't think language can fail
Fail to do what
You wouldn't ask experience to be language
You wouldn't mop with a tennis ball
I think poets are the best kind of people
and experience is not very abstract to me

The memory of the morning after
I slept with Paul starts blank then
I remember light coming through the blinds
hitting the towel still in the guest bed
of the vacation rental house
empty of decoration
except a few pieces of sports memorabilia
like the bedroom of a suicidal Tom Brady fan
Have you seen *A Star Is Born*
I asked him
each time he fell back to sleep
to force him to wake up again and pay attention to me
when he was getting dressed I asked him
if he'd seen *A Star Is Born* so he would stop

I would not want to be an angel
of the lower orders
so assigned the role of guardian or worse
property angel
I think I'd quit that job too
I was thinking of wrought iron and black denim
because I was thinking of angels
because I was thinking of an Eileen Myles reading
I went to 6 years ago under a sky also very black
The specific dark and the specific and unvaried
glamour of the people in line outside the church
made me afraid of domestic things like
shutting my cat in a closet and leaving him there all night
or growing tired of the man I loved

Getting off the train at Botanic Garden
in the onslaught of new air I had escaped New York
I got out and hadn't I wanted to
It felt like I could go
I saw it work
when nothing would budge
I did not put my favorite thing in a poem
I pressed my thumbs into John's palms
to draw the circles I always drew there
I have been someone I don't want around
The spirit matter has rolled between the hills
like thunder
The gate at that station looked like the imaginary gate
where in old poems things happened and stories began

Brittany and I had to work our way backward
What my brain wants
is to go into the space between everything
but we worked our way
from the problem of worthlessness
and the lack of proof we deserve to live
to the solution which is the poem that can think
My ex-husband will not talk to me but sends poems about death
I look at only briefly since real death is in my life
and asks which translators of Proust I like
I say Moncrieff and Kilmartin not because I don't care
because I like the basic ones the most
the ones with flowers the ones that know one day
we'll find out what happened at the party did matter

BABY BLUE

Until I devised a ritual for accepting the cruelty inside me
I could not sleep and looked for a thin red candle

And to see what his name in the vernacular of poets stands for
I read the Wikipedia page for Vaslav Nijinsky once and for all

The name is used when love is fate
When what is loved is hurt

When you storm from the room
When you'll never dance again

When John's friend died he wrote a song
Julie waved her hands in front of her eyes when she spoke it

A name that goes on a thin red candle
The famous image of David Koresh paused on the TV screen

So I could tell everyone I had two revelations by the time I was thirty
When his cousin on A&E said God was going to use him for things

The word "use" lit up and I wondered why
God, when it is assumed, is assumed to be total

I drew a diagram for Kyle of a world on a legal pad
Where roughly half of the stick figures on the curve of Earth are in relation to God

The other half has no connection and neither half knows which they are
Why not something like that I said

Kyle lifted the flannel shirt off my back and began tracing letters on my skin
From shoulder blade to shoulder blade and crossing my spine

W-A-C-O
F-B-I S-U-C-K-S

And in my dream when I did sleep Ben told me he had not stopped thinking
In his spell the clove that stood for us had not diminished like the others

Jeesoo started speaking in tongues in the group chat
I texted her directly but the riddles did not stop

My mother took rocks from the grief counselor's bowl
The placard at the museum acknowledged partial, fractional, and promised gifts

Shy said I could write a long poem like a movie
The night I heard all the wrong songs

Butt-dialed in high school by the boys in the basement I heard the one I loved
Ask the group if they believe in magic

The night my sister's boyfriend shot a gun into the bayou
I stood on the pier snarling and horrible, typing messages on my phone

Near the emergency stairwell at the casino I split a snack-size bag of pretzels
With Charlie during the worst fight of my life

The tree twitched—every tree twitched
I heard Peter's favorite song vibrating through the cold car window

Peter who is dead now but used to spit in the wind on a boat
Climb the walls when the police came

His family's business ruined by the hurricane, the oil spill, the year he died, the spring
I ripped a gold strip off a silver box

A book of matches ruined by the dew
Phone on silent lit up green, each thing was two

I listened for the song echoing in the parking garage
I needed an answer now

At the haunted house my boyfriend got paid to chase families with a chainsaw
In my mother's bed he predicted his lazy eye would ruin his future

Told me he was reading the Stoics
Showed me photos of his daughter on his phone

The last time I saw Peter he was swaying on the porch of a restaurant
Saying you're the best, you've always been the best

Showing me photos on a silver digital camera of Dubrovnik, Croatia
Where his family came from, his last name with too many consonants

I'm a Skrmetta
I came from the most beautiful place in the world

My sister told me what she had seen in the corner
Wine teeth, winter

Birds restless at night, rotten fruit in the bowl
Strangely colored gnats, ravens circling in pairs

My mom's greasy Yorkies shrieking
Thick black vapor rising from the earth

I got in the pool, my mom came out of my aunt's house and got in the pool
Her friend Christine who used to be named Debbie

Who we still accidentally call Debbie
Who dated one of the boys from ZZ Top

Who was a Camel cigarette girl
Who buried cases of Camel cigarettes the size of coffins in Sonja's backyard

Came out of the house and got in the pool
Floating stomach up while someone passed around a vape pen

Called it brass knuckles
The white coffin of purity

I was trying so hard to believe it
Beat myself up trying

Before she dunked her head underwater my mom said
I saw a thousand swirling termites and one dead frog

Certain people are not like birds
They are like numbers of birds, like numbers of consonants

And the huge flaw from childhood I retain
Acknowledges the huge flaw from childhood you retain

KATELYN

I sent these behemoth emails

Charlie Morgan from college

Nobody ever loved him

Said he did not believe I was a moral relativist

But I never said what I was

Because I'm not a complete idiot

Brain surgery and rocket science amount to the same

It's another spoiled quest

And you aren't even from Rome

If anyone wanted to respond he'd have to print the email out and carry it

The conversation grown dark and staggered

Don't worry, you're going to see perfect blue

If not on Merritt Parkway, then somewhere else

So an angel did once alight in my breast

He was not the nice kind of person you'd expect

He wrote a hundred chapters about mornings

The idea for his work came with a rolled ankle in the Guermantes driveway

I made the mistake of talking about Frank O'Hara

To my mother in the car that night

As if pigeons could've flown in different directions

KATELYN

Nebraska was corn

The poems forked as a devil road

Poems with tines like lightning on a dead brain

You will sometime be struck by the force of longing in the nighttime

Its being incommensurate with the day's manageable feelings

As disparate as actual night and actual day

Science works only as well as its lowliest practitioner

And they didn't fingerprint the grass

Snails stand for primordial chaos

The slug that came to eat our dinner had nothing to live for

Nothing to fear

I didn't mean you when I said someone has to live in Ohio

I think I could just barely push here

Hell will not enclose your tragedy

I'm a mandated reporter

And it won't end at cursed shapes

ONE-DAY WINNING STREAK

Things fell apart at dinner. Everyone hunting for the lie which I found.
Don't hate me because I was a child prodigy. I was a new being
wrought from chaos just like everybody else.
I grew up in Beverly Hills the same as you, a blue raspberry filter on the lens.
Now my job making fake paintings for TV is beautiful.
In terms of filmmakers I like who everyone likes,
but you can't speak to the dead or the very famous.
I built a world that looked like this one, but it bombed.

Having these thoughts while the lake flickers was a waste of scenery.
The pointlessness of gathering information surprised me when I laid every piece of it
on the picnic table made of perforations and rust, weeks of what you said.

I had done nothing for the approach.
Language was a material. My dumbest friend said that.
A song of any sort would've been an approach.

I believe in anything you could say about art, knowing the metaphysical world
could not be how I imagine it is why I imagine it.
I've never been too drunk to dream, the supernatural angelic battle going on
while I sit on David's lap while John crushes a Vyvanse
while the last bits he rubs around his teeth dissolve,
saying I love you was my favorite way to pass the time.

I wanted to feel like I was being passed around,
mobile as a fallen angel so then I'd have to be one.
I'm not in the wrong I'm in New York submitting to the feeling
of knots getting untied by time, matches saying strike gently.
My mom's ex-boyfriend's ex-wife left voicemails in the middle of the night.
We listened over breakfast in bands of sunlight.

Rainbows in the hose water, halos where it ricocheted off the chicken wire.
The way she said "slut" was love for the wrong reasons.

I stopped reading horoscopes because they assume we want to get better.
I never panicked about the millennium beyond whatever I got secondhand. Why
anyone would chase anything they could catch is the lie.

LAST NIGHT KYLE

Last night Kyle sang into the camera on his phone
I had a vision of getting into a truck with him late at night harrowed
because someone somewhere far away but close enough to drive
was in the middle of dying and thought about hot girl summer
how I realized if I gave myself over to trying
I could predict the death of every person I loved
and I would've sworn I had no central delusion there, on the street
Kevin Killian had just died
I thought I'll stop and look into this churchyard
a stone angel leaned on a cross of different stone
bothered by the sound of flowers smashing together in the breeze
I was overcome with some rosy-fingered feeling
that poets are worth double or more
or the hole is different
This was the graveyard edit
No one said *hey Courtney that was pretty scary are you okay*
Least of all myself
I went from door to door making non-profound confession
the yarrow stalks my witness
the water on the curtain of the carriage
You're supposed to find the person you could never be mean to
Bring them to meet your ancestors in the mausoleum
In the bathtub I read about the ravine
In the ravine I read about the bathtub
Never found the cool
Both sides of the rock being hot
I was thinking of all the angels ever fallen
When the cards were a little hard to read I got new ones
The spirit world rose toward me in everything
in the blue hat I saw on the platform

in the backward song
Garbage bags burned
I was always able to see the other life
but not this one

UPSTAIRS BAR

Without a crush and an enemy I am nothing
My death grip and sense of ritual
reflect these values
In a voice so loud I read the role
of Agamemnon while Jessa rolls her eyes
which are so doll-like in their blue
and roundness she can't wear dresses
rolls them because she's wearing man's
dreadful will in the scabbard of her body
like a blade because I said she had to
to make a sort of complicated joke of betrayal
when she falls in love with Andy

and at work Eric got so mad because Charlotte said,
when he asked what she wanted to do, nothing
so he came running over to me, the nearest adult
repeating the entire thing and added everything
has to be something and I remembered what the note meant
in my phone that says "scene of us eating breakfast
listening to voicemail," it meant whatever love there was
for the right reasons wasn't any more desirable
than love for the wrong ones

and on Sterling Darcy picks up a plastic box from the ground
thick Lucite with a triangular opening
on the way to hear the Colombian band
in the park where I'll lie on my back
and think how I haven't done this in a while
I take it from her, hold it up to the sky
and touch the three points of the triangle

in a pattern that feels like it comes up from the ground
Darcy says *Okayyyyy?* I know
I don't know what that was about
but it felt ancient

Drama of bringing my ex-husband a book
when he went to bed thinking of deformation/
mutation so it's funny I sent that, he says
What do you mean by geometry tho
I say the physical plane we are on is made of space
while we are sloppy beings of time, the geometry
of time is like trying to map a swamp
because of memory
Then put my phone away

When I am worried I am a shit artist I tell myself
language is the instrument not the voice
but instruments don't do anything by themselves
so it's not like an instrument
it's only like itself
so I try to meet it and if that's enough
I deserve to live even if
I can't get the thing to come out of the underworld
You can laugh but it took
You can laugh because you laugh or you'll cry
That's what Kim used to say to her patients
when she gave them a bath

Years later a fake conversation with a man in LA
in which I've already resigned to a spell
where all the spell wants like anyone else is to continue
You're making art now. That's amazing. That's great.
What I wanted most of all was for him to describe me

like when an ad is inspiring in spite of what it really is
Buildings made sense
Did a fight make sense
It made sense to continue
No sand book
No book of the dead
though it says
on giving a mouth to the deceased
on giving a mouth to the deceased
of not letting the heart of the deceased be taken away
from him in the underworld

In the yard an actor named Michael Patrick stared aggressively into my eyes
even though I told the most boring story I could think of
and suddenly being an actor seemed a terrible affliction
where every moment you obsess over what it means to be a person
physically instead of just mentally, emotionally, and psychically
and the orbs of light of varying strengths balled up around
string lights, the stray tiki torches and green citronella flame
described something oracular and tragic as fate
which I of course became aware of much later
when I sang the second chorus
awaited the bridge and the third

TALKING

Martin knows numbers are emotional but can't explain

Instead he writes til til til in black paint

Most poems want way too much

To feel, to know the feeling, to know what it means to feel it, then to learn

It won't happen in this world

With its nine circles of hell

And angels having numeric values

The second lowest order of angels

An embarrassment

And I love to say "why do you hate me" like a baby bird

To whoever but most when it's you

That guy always has egret feathers in his hand

I was on my knees laying small cots on the linoleum

When through the tempered glass I saw you seeing me in the middle of my work

My love for you was like singing insofar as it made no sense

Because as I understand it

It making no sense to sing is what singing is about

Minushka entered the chat meowing by Logan's window

Who explained it's a sad sound but I don't know why she's sad

And showed me a drawing of a box of fruit in a market

And said his brain gave him the idea

The children are beginning to understand a lot happens there

I had a dream in my head

A fortune, a prong

I didn't tell them when we looked at portraits

We'd have to believe in regret

Emma often works on a conceptual plane

I tell her mother as she empties huge cans of Hunt's tomatoes into a blender

About the fifty or so dandelion puffs she put on a large leaf

Like a plate and explained the people who came to the playground could make wishes

And the feather and rock I removed from her shoe which made her cry

Because I didn't even ask, she screamed, I didn't even ask what they were for

Animals aren't magic

Johnny held a dead beetle up to the camera

Manipulated its wings for twenty minutes instead of talking

I tell Martin's mother I have never met anyone like Martin because I haven't

And she begins to cry because she knows what I mean

And her husband puts his hand on her shoulder

Martin said he wanted to write his autobiography:

At zero he lived near Riverside Park

At one he lived near Riverside Park

At two he thought he would always be two

I didn't know I would ever be three, he said laughing

So he taught me how to say what being young was like

Elmo being three and a half years old

Was the bombshell of the *Sesame Street* town hall on CNN

If Elmo were my student I would observe his speech patterns

And delayed adoption of the first-person pronoun instead of his name

Which would make sense for a younger child

In Reggio Emilia they threw a system away

Without knowing what the new one would look like

Beyond the fact that we would pay attention

Honoring the basic mode of love

Taking extensive notes on the way a child responds to materials

A change of materials in response, taking more notes

And Pasolini went to school there

And he made the *Trilogy of Life*

And I used to joke that my dog would solve his murder

And I used to think I didn't care about *The Canterbury Tales*

In the chat Martin wrote UNMUTE

I WANT TO BE THE ONLY PERSON WHO TALKS IN THIS MEETING

TALK TO ME RIGHT NOW

Which we ignored

Then he started unmuting himself and saying "I love you"

As a form of sabotage because he knew we would be unable to ignore him

We'd have to stop and say "I love you too"

We figured out why Jacob didn't want to talk to me anymore

He could never stop thinking how I'd soon say goodbye

The truth is I behaved in a way I don't want to be remembered for

A fortune, a prong

I forgot to write down who wrote the poem that says

Be something perfect that doesn't count and change but

You do count, are always changing

Still it's what I think you are

2008

After the shrimp festival under bug glow

little moving pieces of light in the pale

light halos responding to my motion

threw rotisserie chicken bones into the

woods that night. The quarter hour alone I

read from the Bible on my phone and thought

is this about me? I went listening, let

words between myself and one who is no

longer in or has not yet entered this world

be few as pure strategy. I was so desperate

for information from outside

the event, like the dark outside the windows

but from outside it was the house that was dark.

In comparing myself to others there was a slippage,

from other bodies to somewhere between

myself and works of art, first a documentary

about a very rare type of mirage. I

was nothing like the mirage and nothing

like the way the men talked about it,

a kind of respectful wonder I doubted I had ever felt.

Then there were the poems I was nothing like.

Kyle reached out having read Ecclesiastes

to his father. I remember you loved

there is a time for casting stones away and a time

for gathering stones together.

From the rectangle of blue light I read all is vanity

all is vanity and a striving after wind and I did

love that but at 90 degrees, sweating

in the middle of the night, my nearly euphoric

fear, how much I didn't know I didn't know,

that one day I would turn around and see

lined up all the things I had done in order to survive

and think what's amazing is not what you did,

not that you did it when you were a little child

but that you did all these sad strange things for me.

I LOVE INFORMATION

If you're hewing the stone it goes pomegranate dove pomegranate dove

I've been watching my boyfriend watch *Pierrot le fou* and I'd like to prolong

The experience of measured green tones in the dark on the contour of his cheek

Pomegranate dove lion palm

Capital chapter column harp

I want to know how to build the tabernacle

Who had daughters who had sons

Gold letters announce the wrestlers

Ropes describe the circle

My friend witnesses a nonconsensual exorcism in her living room

Steels herself in the doorway of her bedroom because the one who hosts the demon

Appears to have died under the forceful grip of the recently baptized

She saw the video attended the brunch bought a clump of daisies

Sewed jewels into her clothes like a Romanov duchess

Dropped the spoon in Brighton Beach

Where I went once but was too high to sit down

I like being told the plot by a friend I like being sung a song on the spot

Words the children are learning

Pistil stamen pistil stamen

What Brittany had for breakfast

Rye sourdough avocado scallion

And I will tell them whatever they want to know

When they swing the light around my head

My hands on the folding table

Beta fish in glass orbs next to Ziploc bags of neon gravel

Ritual bath indicating the purity of beginning

But this one is drinking whiskey from a red frosted tumbler

Under the crown molding painted red

Sending a text about her own desperation

With the necessary provisional belief that this time

The words will do something they can't

Razor falling on tile

He said she said TV isn't working to its full potential with color

But I watch the *Ozark* pilot like it's a painting

I'd dedicate my life to any chronicle if I thought it could be complete

An undercover Russian officer at the bottom of the stairs

Writes about who goes up them

Knows they will come down

It's not you it's me

I heard a man on the Upper West Side say more like a character than a person

Into his phone I am suffering and I am looking up

For someone to reach down to help me

They are there and sort of paying attention but I can't get them to understand

I'm afraid the path I'm on

Without help

If I continue

Is going to destroy me

I said hello to the doorman and went to work

The implication that nonfiction is supposed to be useful

Stems from the implication that information is supposed to be

A painting is better proof

A song is the best proof but you can't be sure they exist unless one is happening

You hand things to each other go to work sell copiers

Night recognizes these people are vulnerable

Lets them rest

Some events like dreams

On a roller coaster with two famous football players

Watching the director of that movie walk between decorative concrete spheres

My teacher said be careful you are veering into the conceptual

If you write about boring things it's going to be boring

Pomegranate dove pomegranate dove

Scientific method by way of Elvis fans who cannot be wrong

Because there are so many of them

Permission to shoot starlings

God turned time back only ten degrees

My husband emerged from his studio wild-eyed

Pupils dilated from the dark

Paint-thinning chemical fumes rolled cartoonlike across the floor

My therapist keeps saying I'm normal

Because I keep telling her I'm not

Pomegranate dove Christmas ornament

I said I don't want to be crazy about the circle

I don't want its center to be everywhere

I'm probably not washing my strawberries properly

There is no good ending but a prophet

Or the kind of person who never dies

Notes

Poems from this book have appeared in *blush_lit*, the *Brooklyn Rail*, *Critical Quarterly*, *Flag + Void*, *Ghost City Review*, *Peach Mag*, *Newest York*, and *Night Music Journal*.

The three-line poem quoted in the first Katelyn poem was written by Mikey Vozick-Seltzer.

Acknowledgments

Thank you to all of my former students. Thank you Milo and Augie.

Thank you Kim, John, and Gabriel Bush.

Thank you Payton Barronian, Anne-Louise Brittain, Will Carington, Jake Goicoechea, Kyle Morgan, Jessa Ross, Rozz Therrien, and Andy Weber for being the content of my life and these poems. I love you.

Thank you Jameson Fitzpatrick, Brittany Miller, and Andrew Stone for being brilliant, generous readers of so many of these poems and for everything you've taught me about writing and art.

Thank you Ben Fama, Zach Halberg, Shy Watson, Jeesoo Lee, and the Cool Memories workshop.

Thank you Anselm Berrigan and Ben Lerner for your support and for being my teachers.

Thank you Brian Teare for selecting my manuscript and for your words.

Thank you to everyone at Milkweed Editions.

photo: Jake Goicoechea

COURTNEY BUSH is the author of *Every Book Is About The Same Thing*. Her films, made with collaborators Jake Goicoechea and Will Carington, have been screened at festivals internationally. She works in childcare and lives in New York.

milkweed
EDITIONS

Founded as a nonprofit organization in 1980, Milkweed Editions is an independent publisher. Our mission is to identify, nurture, and publish transformative literature, and build an engaged community around it.

Milkweed Editions is based in Bdé Óta Othúŋwe (Minneapolis) within Mní Sota Makhočhe, the traditional homeland of the Dakhóta people. Residing here since time immemorial, Dakhóta people still call Mní Sota Makhóčhe home, with four federally recognized Dakhóta nations and many more Dakhóta people residing in what is now the state of Minnesota. Due to continued legacies of colonization, genocide, and forced removal, generations of Dakhóta people remain disenfranchised from their traditional homeland. Presently, Mní Sota Makhóčhe has become a refuge and home for many Indigenous nations and peoples, including seven federally recognized Ojibwe nations. We humbly encourage our readers to reflect upon the historical legacies held in the lands they occupy.

milkweed.org

Milkweed Editions, an independent nonprofit publisher, gratefully acknowledges sustaining support from our Board of Directors; the Alan B. Slifka Foundation and its president, Riva Ariella Ritvo-Slifka; the Amazon Literary Partnership; the Ballard Spahr Foundation; *Copper Nickel*; the McKnight Foundation; the National Endowment for the Arts; the National Poetry Series; and other generous contributions from foundations, corporations, and individuals. Also, this activity is made possible by the voters of Minnesota through a Minnesota State Arts Board Operating Support grant, thanks to a legislative appropriation from the arts and cultural heritage fund. For a full listing of Milkweed Editions supporters, please visit milkweed.org.

Interior design by Mary Austin Speaker
Typeset in Sabon

Sabon was designed in the 1960s for a group of German printers seeking printing consistency across Monotype and Linotype hot metal typesetting machines. Sabon's roman and italic attributes, respectively, were modeled after 16th-century typefaces designed by Claude Garamond and Robert Granjon. One of the first texts to use Sabon was the limited-edition Washburn College Bible, composed in thought-unit typography by designer Bradbury Thompson and featuring frontispieces by Josef Albers in 1979. Sabon was also used to print the *Book of Common Prayer* used by the Episcopal Church, as well as their secondary liturgical texts, such as the *Book of Occasional Services* and *Lesser Feasts and Fasts*.